HISTORY IN PICTURES

World War Two

WAR IN THE PACIFIC

Robert Hamilton

Trans
Atlantic
Press

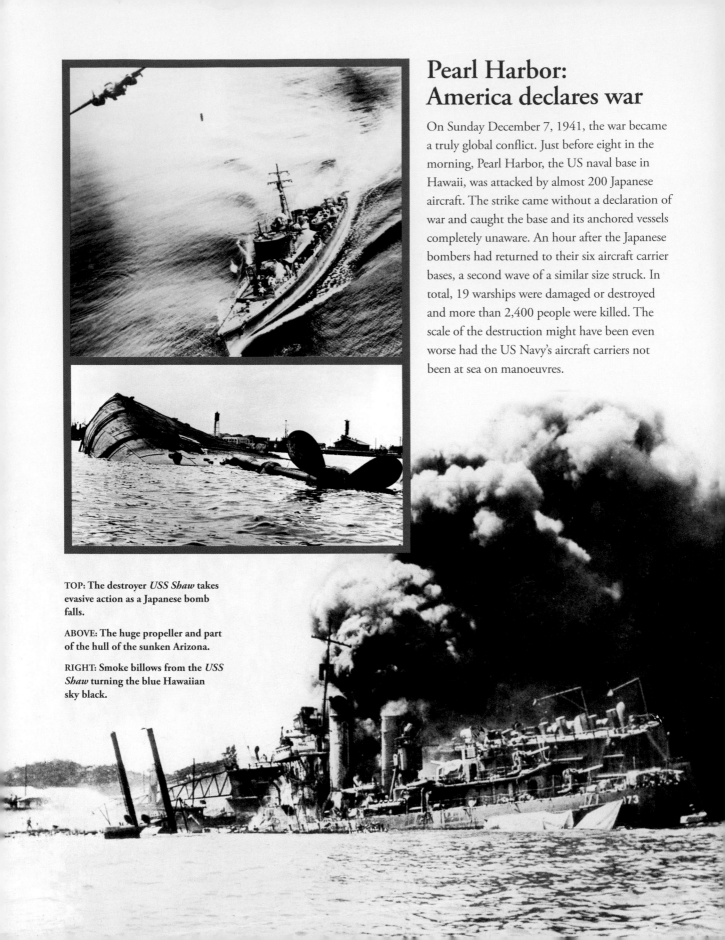

Pearl Harbor: America declares war

On Sunday December 7, 1941, the war became a truly global conflict. Just before eight in the morning, Pearl Harbor, the US naval base in Hawaii, was attacked by almost 200 Japanese aircraft. The strike came without a declaration of war and caught the base and its anchored vessels completely unaware. An hour after the Japanese bombers had returned to their six aircraft carrier bases, a second wave of a similar size struck. In total, 19 warships were damaged or destroyed and more than 2,400 people were killed. The scale of the destruction might have been even worse had the US Navy's aircraft carriers not been at sea on manoeuvres.

TOP: The destroyer *USS Shaw* takes evasive action as a Japanese bomb falls.

ABOVE: The huge propeller and part of the hull of the sunken Arizona.

RIGHT: Smoke billows from the *USS Shaw* turning the blue Hawaiian sky black.

Japan's pre-emptive strike

Tension between the United States and Japan had been mounting for some years. Japan desired to be the dominant power in East Asia and the declining colonial presence of Britain, France and the Netherlands in the region had made this a real possibility. However, the United States, with its presence in the Philippines and interests in the resources of the East Indies, continued to pose a major hurdle. Japan felt squeezed by the United States since Washington had imposed an oil embargo and aided China in the Sino-Japanese War in response to Japan's aggressive expansionism. Attempts to reach a diplomatic solution to the dispute failed, since Roosevelt was anxious not to be seen as appeasing Japan in the manner that Hitler had been by Britain and France prior to the invasion of Poland.

By November 1941, Japan's fuel supplies were running dangerously low so its navy resolved to capture the oilfields of the Dutch East Indies. Fearing that the United States would declare war as a result and convinced that a war was inevitable, Japanese pilots launched a pre-emptive strike on the US fleet.

TOP: A line of Japanese battleships with the Mitsu nearest the camera.

MIDDLE ABOVE: A massive cloud of smoke rises after the first wave of attacks, making accurate bombing more difficult. A Japanese plane can just be made out through the smoke.

MIDDLE BELOW: The USS Arizona sinks, engulfed in smoke and flames.

LEFT: The Japanese attack on Pearl Harbor severely disabled the US Pacific Fleet, allowing Japan to push into Southeast Asia with little opposition.

Southeast Asia falls to Japan

The conflict in the Pacific escalated rapidly. On December 10, 1941 the British navy suffered an appalling blow when two of its largest battleships, the *Repulse* and the *Prince of Wales*, were sunk by Japanese bombers. Japan made several lightning-fast strikes throughout the area, and by the end of the year the US bases at Guam and Wake Island had been captured. Hong Kong fell on Christmas Day. Japanese forces moved swiftly in an attempt to seize control of Southeast Asia following the attack on Pearl Harbor and their run of victories in Malaya, Hong Kong, Thailand and the Philippines. They now launched attacks throughout the Pacific; in January 1942, Manila, the Dutch East Indies, Kuala Lumpur and Burma were all invaded.

TOP: Scenes during a battle just off Guadalcanal in December 1942. 33 Japanese planes attacked an American convoy but 32 of them were shot down. Here a bomb has just landed next to the American cruiser, *San Francisco* but the attacking aircraft has been successfully gunned down and plummets into the sea leaving a thick trail of smoke.

RIGHT: American scout-bombers and units from the Pacific Fleet working together in patrol operations in March 1942.

OPPOSITE BELOW: A Japanese soldier during a skirmish in Burma.

OPPOSITE ABOVE: A scout group of British, American, Chinese and native Kachin troops wades through a river in the Burmese jungle.

Withdrawing from Burma

This put the Allies under immense pressure. British troops in Malaya were forced to retreat to Singapore by February. The city fell on February 15, and about 80,000 British and Australians were captured. Later in February, Japan attacked Australia itself, bombing the northern city of Darwin. Then the Japanese landed on the island of Java on February 26, defeating British and Dutch naval forces in the Battle of the Java Sea. By early spring, it seemed that the Japanese were almost invincible. British troops had been forced to withdraw across the mainland of Burma towards the Indian border, and the Japanese were continuing to capture islands throughout the western Pacific.

Japan and China

The Second Sino-Japanese War, July 1937–September 1945, was the largest Asian war in the 20th century. It also made up more than 50% of the casualties in the Pacific War, if the 1937-1941 period is taken into account.

From December 1937, events such as the Japanese attack on the USS Panay and the Nanking Massacre swung public opinion in the West sharply against Japan, increasing fear of Japanese expansion. This in turn prompted the United States, the United Kingdom and France to provide loan assistance for war supply contracts to the Republic of China. Furthermore, Australia prevented a Japanese government-owned company from taking over an iron mine in Australia, and banned iron ore exports in 1938. Japan retaliated by invading and occupying French Indochina (present-day Vietnam, Laos and Cambodia) in 1940, and successfully blockaded China from the import of arms, fuel and 10,000 tons per month of materials supplied by the Allies through the Haiphong-Yunnan Fou railway line.

To pressure the Japanese to end all hostilities in China, the United States, Britain and the Dutch East Indies began oil and steel embargos against Japan. The loss of oil imports made it impossible for Japan to continue operations in China. This chain of events set the stage for Japan to launch a series of military attacks against the Allies following the raid on Pearl Harbor by the Imperial Japanese Navy on December 7, 1941.

BELOW: One of the US Navy's amphibious trucks brings supplies ashore at New Caledonia in the South Pacific. American troops landed on the Free French island-colony in April 1942.

RIGHT: A senior officer from the Chinese army salutes wounded troops after the North Hunan battle in July 1942.

ABOVE: A Chinese machine-gunner in position ready for attack, July 1942

TOP: Chinese soldiers stride out in March 1942.

America's first victories in the Pacific

The Battle of the Coral Sea took place on May 4-7, 1942. American aircraft carriers off New Guinea intercepted a Japanese invasion force heading towards Papua and the southern Solomon Islands. This was the first naval battle in which all the fighting was done by the pilots of planes launched from aircraft carriers; it was also the first defeat for the Japanese. There were losses on both sides, but the Japanese fleet was turned back with the sinking of one of its aircraft carriers, making the Coral Sea America's first victory in the war with Japan.

ABOVE: American GIs
manning a Howitzer
launch an attack on
Japanese troops in Burma.

RIGHT: Speeding at
treetop level, a US
Douglas A20 attack-
bomber strafes.

OPPOSITE: Marines board
an LCM landing craft in
the Aleutian Islands before
setting off to push the
Japanese off Kiska Island.

Midway and Guadalcanal

One month later, four more Japanese aircraft carriers were destroyed in the Battle of Midway, severely reducing their capabilities. This heralded a clear change in the Allies' fortunes in the Pacific theatre: the balance of both air and sea power was now tipping in favour of the Allied forces. Allied attacks were launched in the Solomon Islands, and the first landings took place at Guadalcanal on August 7. At first Allied forces met little resistance, but the Japanese troops were very swiftly reinforced and fierce fighting was to rage for the rest of 1942. Naval battles also continued with the Americans inflicting further heavy damage to the Japanese navy and to a supply convoy off Guadalcanal in November. The island was finally won in February 1943 at a cost of thousands of lives. Within days, the Americans moved to assist the Australians in pushing the Japanese out of New Guinea. The Australians had already dealt the Japanese their first defeat of the war at Milne Bay in September 1942 and with the additional US forces they were able to win back control of the island by the end of 1943.

TOP AND MIDDLE: Pilots in America were on constant standby in case of an attack on their shores.

LEFT: Americans gather to enrol for the US Air Force in New York.

OPPOSITE ABOVE: Men of Britain's 14th Army patrol through swamps in Burma.

OPPOSITE BELOW: US Navy scout bombers circle in formation above their aircraft carrier home in the Pacific in November 1942.

Dwight "Ike" Eisenhower

After the Japanese attack on Pearl Harbor, Eisenhower was assigned to the General Staff in Washington, where he served until June 1942 with responsibility for creating the major war plans to defeat Japan and Germany. He was appointed Deputy Chief in charge of Pacific Defenses before becoming Chief of the War Plans Division. He was then appointed Assistant Chief of Staff in charge of Operations Division under Chief of Staff General George C. Marshall, who spotted talent and promoted accordingly.

In 1942, Eisenhower was appointed Commanding General, European Theater of Operations and was based in London. In November, he was also appointed Supreme Commander Allied Force of the North African Theater of Operations. In February 1943, his authority was extended as commander of AFHQ across the Mediterranean basin to include the British 8th Army which was under the command of General Bernard Montgomery.

ABOVE: The assignment of Brigadier General Dwight D. Eisenhower (left) to be Chief of The General Staff's War Plans Division was disclosed on February 19 by the War Department. Eisenhower succeeded Major General Leonard T. Gerow (right), who was shifted to command of the 29th Division.

LEFT: This is one of the first pictures to be received in Britain of the US Flying Fortress, which had been in action against the Japanese in the Philippines. Here the pilots are seen consulting a map beside their giant machine.

LEFT: The camp at Manzanar, California, that housed more than 60,000 Japanese citizens and Japanese Americans during the war.

ABOVE: US Ordnance crew loading up a Boeing Flying Fortress of the Hawaiian Air Force Bomber Command in March 1942; they are seen carefully handling a 300-pounder.

ABOVE: US air mastery on Guadalcanal.
'Wildcat' fighter planes lined up and ready
for US Navy and Marine pilots at an airfield
on Guadalcanal Island. Although US Marines
had withdrawn from the Island, the Marine
Air Force was still there fighting hard with
Army and Navy pilots. Up until February the
Japanese had lost 876 planes – five times that
of the American losses.

Allied offensives in the Pacific, 1943–44

Midway proved to be the last great naval battle for two years. The United States used the ensuing period to turn its vast industrial potential into actual ships, planes, and trained aircrew. At the same time, Japan, lacking an adequate industrial base or technological strategy, a good aircrew training program, or adequate naval resources and commerce defense, fell further and further behind. In strategic terms the Allies began a long movement across the Pacific, seizing one island base after another. Not every Japanese stronghold had to be captured; some, like Truk, Rabaul, and Formosa, were neutralized by air attack and bypassed. The goal was to get close to Japan itself, launch massive strategic air attacks, improve the submarine blockade, and finally (only if necessary) execute an invasion.

In November 1943 US Marines sustained high casualties when they overwhelmed the 4,500-strong garrison at Tarawa. This helped the Allies to improve the techniques of amphibious landings, learning from their mistakes and implementing changes such as thorough pre-emptive bombings and bombardment, more careful planning regarding tides and landing craft schedules and better overall coordination.

The US Navy did not seek out the Japanese fleet for a decisive battle, as Mahanian doctrine would suggest, and as Japan hoped; the Allied advance could only be stopped by a Japanese naval attack, which oil shortages, induced by submarine, attack made impossible.

ABOVE: General Frank Merrill and
some of his staff discuss new methods
to hamper the Japanese headquarters
somewhere in the Burmese jungle.

OPPOSITE ABOVE: American soldiers
waving a greeting from one of the
convoy ships arriving at an Australian
port, with thousands of U.S. troops and
war materials in June1942.

OPPOSITE BELOW: Native stretcher
bearers in New Guinea rest themselves
and their casualties in the shade of a
coconut grove en route from the front
lines near Buna to hospitals in the rear.
In skirmishes and large engagements,
United States troops killed over a
thousand Japanese in five days.

Ambushing Japanese troops

The Japanese invasion of Burma in 1942 had successfully cut off supply routes to China along the Burma Road and placed Japanese troops dangerously close to the Indian border. Japanese commanders had hoped that Indian forces in the area would revolt against the British. However, although some captured soldiers were formed into an army to fight against the Allies, colonial Indian divisions, which had fought alongside British troops in North Africa, were redeployed to Burma in 1943, where they fought with great distinction. Now under the overall command of Lord Mountbatten, British troops were reinforced and received greater air support, enabling them to maintain defensive positions deep in the Burmese jungles; the employment of guerrilla tactics would result in some successful campaigns against the Japanese. Major General Orde Wingate formed and led the 77th Indian Infantry Brigade, otherwise known as the Chindits, which adopted the tactic of 'Long Range Penetration', operating in columns deep inside enemy territory, sabotaging infrastructure and ambushing Japanese troops. Although they were eventually ordered to withdraw, as air-drops became more difficult, the Chindits had proved that damage could be inflicted on the Japanese in difficult jungle territory.

1944: Japan in retreat

The hard-won success of Guadalcanal led to a determined advance, codename Operation Cartwheel, by Allied forces through the Solomon Islands and New Guinea during 1943. Japanese forces had a major HQ in the town of Rabaul on the island of New Britain, garrisoned by approximately 100,000 troops, and this now became a strategic goal for the Allies in the Pacific Campaign. In the Battle of Tarawa, a heavily fortified atoll that held the key to the recapture of the Marianas, the Allied beach landings in November were met by the first heavy Japanese resistance at the beachhead to date; this would provide useful experience for future Allied landings such as Iwo Jima – but with a high cost in casualties. In the game of chess played out in the Pacific Islands, the steady pushing of the Allied forces could only have one conclusion, but the delaying tactics of the totally committed Japanese Imperial Army made progress slow and the loss of life very high – on both sides. Nevertheless the first months of 1944 proved the tide had turned on Japan.

ABOVE: US Marines attack a Japanese strongpoint during the landing at Tarawa, where some of the 'bloodiest fighting of the campaign took place', to establish an Allied bridgehead on this central Pacific base. Two Marines – barely visible in their camouflaged cloaks – can be seen crouching behind the shattered stumps of palm trees, having tossed dynamite sticks seen exploding on the Japanese strongpoint.

OPPOSITE: Marines on the littered beach at Tarawa covered their ammunition and other gear with camouflaged shelter-halfs in case the Japanese tried an air attack.

LEFT: A sub-machine gun in one hand and a grenade in the other, a soldier marches at the head of his men in pursuit of Japanese defenders of New Britain Island in the southwest Pacific. US troops, in a two-pronged drive, advanced to new positions on the north and south coasts of New Britain and by March 27, 1944 were less than 170 miles away from the major Japanese base at Rabaul.

Advance of the Marines

OPPOSITE ABOVE: Marines advance across desolate Darry Island in the wake of fleeing Japanese, as the Marines took Eniwetok Atoll in the Marshall Islands. The palm trees were either uprooted or defoliated by the bombardment before the leathernecks came ashore to clean out the holed-up Japanese in February 1944.

OPPOSITE BELOW: American assault troops splash across a shallow stream, near Aitape, where they formed small patrol groups to seek out Japanese defenders of the coastal base on Northern Guinea. US amphibious forces stormed ashore at Aitape and at two points flanking Hollandia, to the west, on April 22, 1944, gaining control of an additional 150 mile stretch of the Northern New Guinea coast for the Allies. Supplementary landings six days later aided in blocking escape routes for an estimated 60,000 Japanese troops entrapped in that area of the southwest Pacific island.

ABOVE: A Japanese soldier, cornered by US Marines on Namur Island, holds out his arms in surrender while another Japanese digs his way out of a blasted blockhouse where twenty Japanese were trapped. An enemy soldier lies dead at the foot of the wrecked stairway (centre). Namur was the northern part of Kwajalein Atoll and one of the Japanese island fortresses in the Central Pacific taken by US forces leading up to the seizure of Kwajalein in the Marshall Islands, February 1944.

The tide turns on Japan

OPPOSITE BELOW: US Marines plunge through the surf at Cape Gloucester, New Britain, after disembarking from a landing craft to push a jeep to shore. An amphibious vehicle nears the beach during landing preparations on the Southwest Pacific island on December 26. Some Marines carry stretchers so that the wounded can be removed promptly to medical stations. US landing forces captured the twin air strips on Cape Gloucester in the initial attacks and then pressed on inland in their campaign against the Japanese.

ABOVE: American Marines wading ashore at Cape Gloucester, New Britain.

OPPOSITE ABOVE: US amphibious tanks line a beach, bringing in supplies to American Marines who landed on Japanese-held Emirau Island in the St. Matthias group of the Southwest Pacific. An amphibious car pulls a truck ashore (left, centre), while in the background, troops form a chain in the surf to convey materials to the beach. US Marines captured the island on March 20, 1944, to complete encirclement of Japanese remnant garrisons on New Britain, New Ireland and the Northern Solomon Islands.

Island-hopping

After securing Guadalcanal and New Guinea in 1943 the Americans continued with their offensives in the Pacific, jumping from island to island, moving ever closer to Japan in a strategy known as 'island-hopping'. In the summer of 1944 the US forces liberated Saipan, Guam and Tinian in the Marianas Island chain, and the invasion of Peleliu and Angaur in the Palau island group followed shortly after. The capture of these islands helped put America's B-29 bombers within range of Japan's main island, and from June 1944 the US Army Air Force began a bombing campaign against Japanese cities, with the intention of forcing the country into submission. In 1945, the bombing became relentless, especially in Tokyo, where thousands of people were killed in firebombing raids; but the Japanese government still refused to surrender.

OPPOSITE ABOVE: A long line of amphibious tanks arrives ashore at Tinian Island in the Marianas chain, August 1944.

RIGHT: American paratroop reinforcements float down from transport planes to a beachhead in support of an amphibious Allied landing on Noemfoor Island, about 100 miles west of Biak Island and 800 miles from the Philippines on July 2, 1944. On the beachhead, vehicles and men of the amphibious force awaited them. The Allies gained control of three Japanese-built airstrips in their five-day capture of the strategic island off the north coast of Netherlands New Guinea. Noemfoor gave the Allies another forward base from which to mount their growing attacks on the enemy.

OPPOSITE BELOW: An American tank patrols Garapan, Saipan's main city. Captured from the Japanese on July 9, 1944 after 24 days of bloody fighting, Saipan was one of the larger Mariana islands, with a substantial civilian population, of which an estimated 22,000 Japanese died. The Japanese garrison numbered 30,000 and was wiped out in the battle, which cost nearly 3,000 American lives with 10,000 wounded.

ABOVE: Installations at the Japanese air base on Woleai Island go up in smoke as planes of a US Navy Carrier task force blast the base during an attack on enemy strongholds in the Western Carolines of the Central Pacific. Planes were wrecked and the airstrip temporarily put out of operation. Surface units and carrier-based aircraft of the American Force sank or damaged 46 Japanese ships, destroyed 160 planes, probably wrecked 54 others and bombed enemy bases during the three-day assault.

Japanese resistance

BELOW: On September 15, US and Australian troops landed on the island of Morotai virtually unopposed; the beaches they chose were unsuited to unloading vehicles and equipment and the troops, including General Douglas MacArthur, had to wade chest-high through the sea. Morotai and its airfield were important to the later invasion of the Philippines and the Japanese knew this well: reinforcements poured into the island and although Allied forces controlled it, Japanese resistance continued until the end of the war, when around 600 remaining troops surrendered.

OPPOSITE: On September 17, US marines haul an anti-tank gun ashore from their landing craft during the invasion of Angaur, another of the Palau islands which had to be taken en route to the Philippines. The small garrison of Japanese fought hard but the battle was over by September 30.

Battle of Peleliu

BELOW: The Battle of Peleliu, one of the small coral islands of Palau, was controversial; the airfield there was of little strategic importance and although the US attackers expected a quick victory, the Japanese had prepared for invasion with great care. From the first landing on September 15, US forces faced determined opposition until November 27 when almost the entire Japanese garrison of 11,000 had been wiped out. This battle was a preview that prepared the US military for similar defensive tactics in Iwo Jima and Okinawa.

OPPOSITE: An iconic photogaph from the war showing a Japanese Torpedo plane crashing in flames as a result of a direct hit from carrier anti-aircraft guns during operations near Saipan in the Marianas.

The Final Battles

BELOW: Seaborne US invasion forces head for the beaches of Iwo Jima on the morning of February 19. The assault on Iwo Jima was a turning point in the Pacific war as Japanese sovereign territory was being invaded for the first time. After capturing the Marianas in 1944, the US was ready to focus on Japan itself. Iwo Jima's three airfields made it a potent attack base for Japanese aircraft and would make it a perfect strategic airbase for assault on Japan. Over 70 days of aerial bombardment preceded the invasion and heavy naval guns pounded the Japanese positions for three days before. In the initial wave, 30,000 US troops landed on the first day.

LEFT: US marines attempt to flush Japanese soldiers out of a cave on Okinawa.

Iwo Jima and Okinawa

Through 1944 into 1945, the Allies were successful in the Far East and Pacific regions, as the Japanese suffered increasingly severe losses both on land and at sea. British and American forces reopened the Burma Road after decimating Japanese forces in June. In the same month, the Battle of the Philippine Sea established Allied naval superiority. The American forces continued 'island hopping' through the Pacific towards Japan, reclaiming the Philippines and enduring some of the worst fighting of the war on Iwo Jima and the Ryukyu Islands, including Okinawa, where fighting was to last for months.

On February 19, 1945 the 3rd, 4th and 5th divisions of the United States Marine Corps staged an amphibious invasion of Iwo Jima, an island some 700 miles south of Tokyo. The fighting was among the fiercest in the Pacific theatre, costing almost 7,000 American lives, making it the deadliest battle in the history of the US Marine Corps. Countless more Japanese died as they defended the island to the death, first engaging the marines in the open and later resisting from hiding places in caves. The battle ended on March 26, by which time 27 American servicemen had performed acts of bravery that would later win them the Medal of Honor.

ABOVE: Realising the strategic importance of the island to the advancing Allies, the Japanese increased the garrison to 18,000 and a defensive plan was initiated. The Japanese commander designed his fortifications to take advantage of the island's topography, especially the extinct volcano Mt Suribachi, where a network of tunnels and gun emplacements enabled the defenders to survive the pulverising American bombardment and to mount a strong defence against infantry attack.

BELOW: Marines of the 4th division storm the shores of Iwo Jima.

Iconic moment on Iwo Jima

BELOW: Five days after the invasion, US forces on Iwo Jima numbered 70,000 and on February 23 a platoon of marines scaled Mt Suribachi and raised the Stars and Stripes at its summit. This moment was captured by photographer Louis R Lowery and achieved iconic status for the American people in general and US forces in particular. The battle would last another month; the last assault by the Japanese being on March 25. Bitter fighting on both sides resulted in many casualties: of the total Japanese military of around 22,000 only a couple of hundred were captured alive - it is assumed the rest died. Of the final number of US troops engaged (110,000), 26,000 became casualties, 7,000 of them fatalities.

Three month battle for Okinawa

In mid-March, as the Battle for Iwo Jima was drawing to a close, the US began the next offensive against the island of Okinawa. At just over 300 miles from Kyushu, the southernmost of Japan's four main islands, Okinawa was to be a springboard for the invasion of Japan proper. After a week long 'softening up' bombardment from the air, US troops of the Tenth Army came ashore largely unopposed. However, the Japanese were lying in wait at better-defended locations and the battle soon became a bloodbath. It took the US almost three months to wrestle control of the island and defeat the Japanese, who once again fought to the death. Unlike Iwo Jima, Okinawa had a large civilian population, which had been warned by Japanese propaganda not to expect any mercy from the Americans. Such scaremongering had terrible consequences; thousands of civilians committed suicide and thousands more died in the fighting. By the end of the battle, an estimated 100,000 Japanese and 12,000 American servicemen had lost their lives.

LEFT: This photograph shows the horrific task the US troops faced on Okinawa, often taking out the Japanese positions one at a time, using explosives and facing suicidal counterattacks that might come without warning. Americans landed on the Island on April 1 and secured it on June 21. In addition to the loss of over 100,000 troops, the Japanese suffered horrific civilian casualties which have never been defined but were estimated between 40-150,000.

ABOVE: Three marines kneel to pray in their fox holes in a rare quiet moment during the Iwo Jima campaign.

OPPOSITE: The capture of the Marianas Islands in 1944 enabled Admiral Nimitz to set up his HQ on Guam with harbour facilities for a third of the US Pacific Fleet. This was followed by the building of Isely Field on Saipan - the first of five airbases in the Marianas which would accommodate the B-29 Superfortresses whose bombs ended the Japanese military regime. Here, more material and machinery are unloaded through the bow doors of LSTs directly onto the quay.

Battle for the Philippines

The United States had shared a close relationship with the Philippines ever since the islands were ceded to Washington at the end of the Spanish-American War of 1898. Thousands of American troops were in the Philippines when the Japanese invaded within hours of the attack on Pearl Harbor. Many were captured and, together with Filipino POWs, they were forced to endure an infamous death march to their internment camp in Bataan. The battle to liberate the Philippines from Japanese rule began on October 20, 1944 when US troops, under the command of General Douglas MacArthur, landed on the island of Leyte. The Japanese attempted to obstruct the landings in what became the largest naval battle of the entire war. The US scored a decisive victory, neutralizing the Japanese navy and allowing US and Australian forces to steadily recapture the Philippines. The Battle for Manila began in February 1945 and ended up being the only major urban battle fought in the Pacific campaign. Fighting was fierce and it took American soldiers more than one month to secure the city. By the time it fell on March 3, thousands of civilians had been killed and the city was almost completely destroyed.

ABOVE: An aerial view of the devastation caused during the fight for Manila. It was to be the only major urban battle of the Pacific campaign.

OPPOSITE ABOVE: Plumes of smoke rise above Manila during fierce fighting between US and Japanese forces in February 1945.

OPPOSITE BELOW: Some of the most intense and ferocious fighting of the Pacific conflict took place as US and Filipino forces battled with the Japanese in the streets of Manila. Battle commenced on February 3 and, after much bloodshed, ended on March 3. The street fighting was reminiscent of Stalingrad and over 100,000 civilians died, either as collateral damage or resulting from deliberate Japanese action. Much of Manila's unique ancient heritage was destroyed as the Japanese defenders used the Intramuros as their bastion. In this picture, a wounded GI is carried by stretcher to a dressing station in City Hall.

Victory in Japan

While victory was being celebrated in Europe, the war against Japan was still raging, but here too the Allies were pushing steadily forward. British forces finally liberated Burma from Japanese control on August 2, 1945, and the American push through the Pacific was bringing US troops gradually closer to Japan.

Roosevelt had died suddenly on April 12 and the new President, Harry Truman, was confronted with the challenging task of winning the war in the Far East. In July 1945, America successfully tested the first nuclear device and it was up to Truman to decide whether this potentially devastating piece of military technology should be used in the Pacific theatre. Truman realized how costly an invasion of the Japanese mainland would be; he had been given a foretaste when an estimated 12,000 Americans died taking Okinawa Island in March. He was also aware that the Allies were exhausted and that many people had lost focus on the Pacific campaign amid the jubilation of the victory in Europe. In addition, the Soviet Union was preparing to declare war on Japan and Truman was keen to stem Stalin's influence in the region. All these considerations encouraged Truman to take the momentous decision to use the bomb.

ABOVE: The scene as troops of the Australian Seventh Division landed east of the Japanese–held Borneo port of Balikpapan, a great oil centre, supported by American ships and aircraft.

OPPOSITE: Irrawaddy rail-head town, Prome, was liberated after a sharp encounter with a few straggling Japanese who held on while the bulk of their troops in the district were wandering aimlessly and defeated around the wild country south of the town. Allied armoured vehicles on the road to Prome were held up by a river crossing.

OPPOSITE ABOVE: Fort Drum, nicknamed the Concrete Battleship, was a defensive installation built on a tiny island in Manila Bay to cover its approaches and the US garrison of Corregidor. The heavily fortified installation bristled with guns and fought hard to resist the Japanese who took it in 1942. When Allied forces recaptured Corregidor in February 1945, Fort Drum remained in the control of the Japanese until April 13, when US forces approached, avoided its heavy guns and landed. A landing craft tanker was called into use and several thousand gallons of an inflammable mixture were poured into the ventilation system and TNT charges set, creating an explosive inferno that wrecked the fort and killed its garrison. In this remarkable photograph, taken by Acme War Pool Correspondent, Stanley Troutman, the LCM can be seen in the foreground while infantry cover the engineers who are feeding the fuel into the vents and setting their charges.

ABOVE: A Japanese tank trap on the beach at Tarakan Island, off the East Coast of Borneo, snares an Australian light tank. Aussie engineers of the Ninth Australian Imperial Forces division try to free it with another tank. A landing craft in the background is made ready to disgorge its valuable cargo.

Invading Borneo

BELOW: Australian forces begin their seaborne landings on the island of Tarakan, Borneo on May 1, 1945. The invasion was well-executed, though there were problems in landing; the Allies had overwhelming numbers by comparison with the Japanese garrison because fierce resistance was expected. Tarakan's oilfields were strategically important and the Allies hoped to make good use of the island's airfield. This picture shows the effectiveness of the modified landing craft that were equipped with rockets; these LCMRs could deliver devastating barrages with lightning speed, just before attacking infantry landed. Pockets of Japanese soldiers held out until June 21.

ABOVE: While conflict subsided in the European and Mediterranean theatres of war, the Allies remained engaged in fierce and deadly combat with Japan in the Far East. Australian troops were fighting in the jungle of New Guinea under the most difficult conditions, resulting in many casualties.

OPPOSITE ABOVE: Ready for emergency a Bren-gunner takes cover alongside the track of the Western Railway at Labuan Island, Borneo to cover the advance of the 9th Division Infantry.

LEFT: A feature of the naval operations off the Sakashima Islands in support of the Okinawa landings was the Japanese suicide aircraft attack. Here, firefighters are busy on board one of H.M. carriers of the British Pacific Fleet after a Japanese suicide plane had crash landed on the flight deck.

OPPOSITE BELOW: Australian soldiers pass the corpse of a dead Japanese soldier killed in the gateway leading to a plantation property on Labuan Island, Borneo.

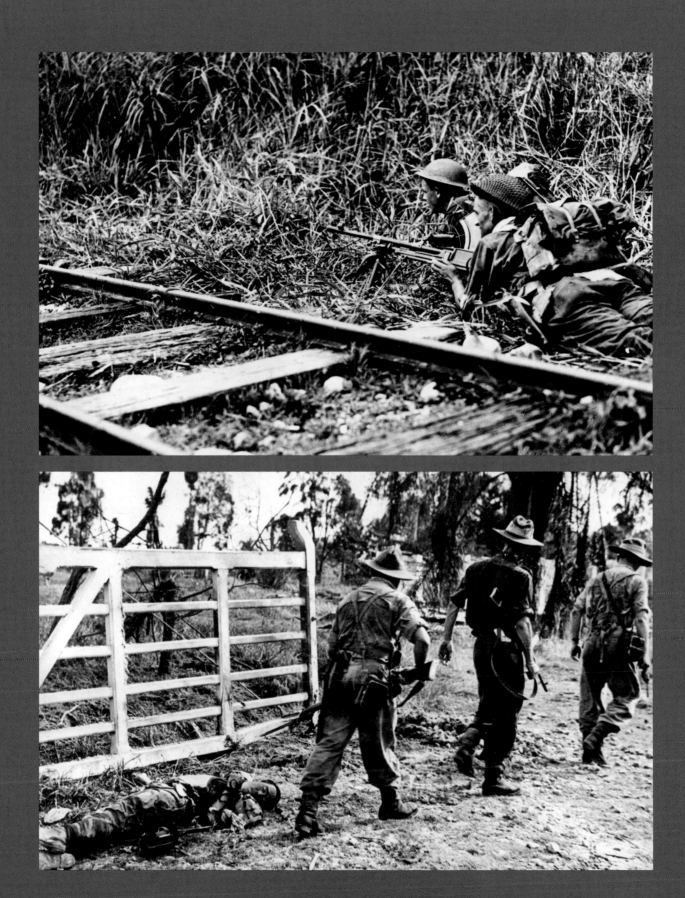

LEFT: The Allied powers called time on the Japanese and sent three B 29 bombers, one of them the Enola Gay, equipped with the 'Little Boy' nuclear device to bomb Hiroshima on August 6, followed by 'Fat Man' dropped on Nagasaki on August 9. The world suddenly became acquainted with the awesome weapon that would dominate military and political reality for generations to come, symbolised in the terrifying mushroom cloud, photographed here over Nagasaki.

OPPOSITE ABOVE: The casing of an atomic bomb of the same type as 'Fat Man', on display in the USA.

OPPOSITE BELOW: Directly under the Hiroshima hypocentre was a modern ferro-concrete building which was one of the few that remained standing after the blast. A dazed survivor wanders the scorched streets of Hiroshima. In the months and years to come the survivors continued to die, many of them from terrible burns and horrible radiation sickness.

BELOW: Nagasaki razed to the ground.

Ultimate weapon unleashed on Japan

An outcome of the Potsdam Agreement was the Potsdam Declaration, which set out the terms for Japan's unconditional surrender. These were sent to the Japanese government by Truman, Churchill and China's President Chiang Kai-shek on July 26. The Japanese government adopted a policy of ignoring the ultimatum because it took away all Japanese sovereignty and reduced its territories as well as threatening the prosecution of war crimes. The response was delivered indirectly by the Japanese Prime Minister in a press conference. The ultimatum was uncompromising in guaranteeing the total devastation of Japan if it did not surrender, but the Imperial forces had no knowledge of the atomic bomb and had already withstood strategic bombing that had destroyed vast areas of some of its cities; the military would rather fight to the death than surrender and leave the Emperor at the mercy of foreign powers.

City of 300,000 vanishes

Hiroshima, Japanese city of 300,000 people, ceased to exist at 9.15 on Monday morning. While going about its business in the sunshine of a hot summer day, it vanished in a huge ball of fire and a cloud of boiling smoke - obliterated by the first atom bomb to be used in the history of world warfare.

Such is the electrifying report of the American crew of the Super-Fortress which dropped the bomb as a cataclysmic warning to the Japs to get out of the war or be destroyed. Hiroshima, the whole crew agreed, was blotted out by a flash more brilliant than the sun.

They told their astonishing story here at Guam to-day. The explosion, they said, was tremendous and awe-inspiring. The words 'Oh my God' burst from every man as they watched a whole city blasted into rubble. Although they were ten miles away from the catastrophe, they felt the concussion like a close explosion of A.A. fire.

The men had been told to expect a blinding flash. They wore special black goggles. Only three of them knew what type of bomb was being dropped. 'It was hard to believe what we saw.' That was how Col. Paul W. Tibbits, pilot of the Super-Fort, described the explosion.

He said: 'We dropped the bomb at exactly 9.15 a.m. and got out of the target area as quickly as possible to avoid the full effect of the explosion. We stayed in the target area two minutes. The smoke rose to a height of 40,000ft.

'Only Captain Parsons, the observer; Major Ferebee, the bombardier; and myself knew what was dropped. All the others knew was that it was a special weapon. We knew at once we had got to get the hell out of there. I made a sharp turn in less than half a minute to get broadside to the target.

'All of us in the plane felt the heat from the brilliant flash and the concussion from the blast. 'Nothing was visible where only minutes before there was the outline of a city, with its streets and buildings and piers clearly to be seen. 'Soon fires sprang up on the edge of the city, but the city itself was entirely obscured.'

OPPOSITE ABOVE: The trio of planes flying towards Hiroshima on August 6 was picked up by Japanese radar and judged to be a reconnaissance flight so no defensive measures were taken. At around 8.15 am, the Little Boy nuclear device exploded about 2,000 feet above the target area in central Hiroshima creating a blaze of light and a shock wave that killed an estimated 70,000 citizens instantly and demolished all of the traditionally constructed buildings in range. In the Enola Gay, co-pilot Robert Lewis asked the question that would be repeated around the world: 'My God, what have we done?'

OPPOSITE BELOW: Both Hiroshima and Nagasaki, though they were important cities for military reasons, were relatively untouched by strategic bombing, which enabled the Manhattan Project's researches to continue in 'real' conditions. Tokyo, pictured, was not so unscathed - fire-bombing had already destroyed vast areas of the capital. The Allies avoided fire-bombing Kyoto but many other Japanese cities such as Nagoya were also devastated, fire-bombs destroying the many wooden buildings, rich with Japan's cultural and religious heritage.

LEFT: A selection of newspapers from across the United States during the week of the bombings.

ABOVE: The devastated city of Tokyo is pictured from the heavily-defended US embassy in September 1945.

This is a Transatlantic Press Book
First published in 2012

Transatlantic Press
38 Copthorne Road, Croxley Green, Hertfordshire, UK

A catalogue record for this book is available from the British Library.

ISBN 978-1-908849-07-6

Printed in China